Can I Talk to Mama?

By:

BILL ROBERTS

WestBow Press books may be ordered through booksellers or by contacting:

WestBow Press
A Division of Thomas Nelson & Zondervan
1663 Liberty Drive
Bloomington, IN 47403
www.westbowpress.com
844–714–3454

Scripture quotations are taken from the Holy Bible, New International Version®, NIV®. Copyright © 1973, 1978, 1984 by Biblica, Inc.™ Used by permission of Zondervan. All rights reserved worldwide.

ISBN: 978–1–6642–9390–8 (sc)
ISBN: 978–1–6642–9391–5 (e)

Library of Congress Control Number: 2023904290

Print information available on the last page.

WestBow Press rev. date: 05/02/2023

WESTBOW
PRESS®
A DIVISION OF THOMAS NELSON
& ZONDERVAN

Foreword

By Bill Roberts

Thank you for taking the time to read this story. Ideally, it should be read while listening to the accompanying song. If you have not heard the song, please go to the site via the QR code on the back of this book and enjoy!

This song/book was a promise to my beloved wife, Mary. Can I Talk to Mama started as a poem to her, then became a song, and is now a children's book. She cried when she read it for the first time. Mary is now in Heaven, and my hope is that everyone who reads this story and listens to this song will be filled with a hope that they will one day be together again with their husband or wife, mom or dad, or someone they love dearly. Thanks be to God! God's blessings to you — Bill Roberts

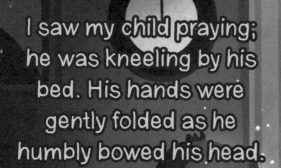

I saw my child praying; he was kneeling by his bed. His hands were gently folded as he humbly bowed his head.

BIBLE

Psalm 5:1–3

He was thanking you for
Jesus with words only
angels hear. He was
thanking you for Heaven
as your Spirit drew near.

Psalm 91:11

In a moment's silence he was deep in words to pray, and I thought for just a minute he was lost on things to say.

Hebrews 11:16

Then with tears that fell like raindrops on a stormy winter's day, I heard him ask You, Father, in his sweetest little boy way.

John 11:35

"Can I talk to Mama? I miss her so much! I miss her kisses and her hugs. I miss her smile; I miss her touch."

Matthew 18:1-5

"Can I talk to Mama? I miss her so much!
The way she tucked me in at night, the
way she kissed and held me tight."

Psalm 34:15

"I know where you're at, Mama. I'll be ok with Dad."

Psalm 34:17–18

"I saw Daddy crying late last night. We miss you, Mama, so much, but we'll be alright."

Isaiah 40:31;
Philippians 3:20–21

"Can I talk to Mama? I miss her so much!

I know she's fine and she's alright, but I wish she was here tonight.

Can I talk to Mama? I miss her so much!

Her eyes, her voice, her hair, her touch, Lord I miss my Mama so much!"

Ecclesiastes 3:1–8; II Corinthians 5:1

"Please grant me, please, just one more wish.

One more hug, one more kiss.

Good night, Jesus.

Good night, Mama.

I love you."

Psalm 40:1-3

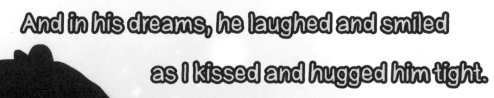

And in his dreams, he laughed and smiled
as I kissed and hugged him tight.

John 15:7–9; Luke 6:21

"I hug and kiss you all the time; I am watching... waiting...you're still mine."

"You know I'm here in Heaven, and the best is yet to come."

"So my child, rest and sleep in peace,
watch over Daddy 'til you come home."

John 1:12

And in the morning, my son woke up with his face stained full of tears.

Philippians 4:6–7; Revelation 7:17

He ran to tell his Daddy as
he held and drew him near.

Psalm 103:11–14

"Daddy, I talked to Mama! She held me in my dreams. She told me that she loved and missed me and she hugged me while she kissed me. She held me in her arms so tight and then she tucked me in last night."

"Daddy, was it real? Was it really as it seemed? He cried and then kissed him and he said she really missed him. She kissed and hugged you tight, then she tucked you in last night."

Romans 10:9–11

"Thank you, Father, for watching over us!

Thank you, Holy Spirit, for the gift of so much love!

Thank you, Jesus!

Thank you, Jesus,

for watching over him!
Thank you!"

About the Author

   Bill Roberts had a miraculous series of
life—changing events in 1983 when he cried
out to God for help. That is another story for
another time. He is the father of three boys,
men now, two of them married with children of
their own. He is married to Martha who loves
Jesus, the church, family, life and of course,
her husband! She encourages Bill every day.

Commentary

Here are the Bible verses that are referenced on each page.

Page 1 – Psalm 5:1-3 – Communication is the key ingredient to any relationship. Likewise, prayer is talking to God personally. We learn from Scripture that God desires a relationship with His creation. Ask God to show you who He is, what He is like, and how He wants you to live. You might be surprised by what prayer and reading the Bible will do for you. The God of the universe wants a deep personal relationship with YOU!

Page 2 – Psalm 91:11 – When we put our trust in God and love Him, the Bible says that angels (another one of God's creations) watch over us everywhere we go. They are there to protect us and to keep us safe.

Page 3 – Hebrews 11:16 – Have you ever felt like things are not quite right? That is probably because we are not in Heaven yet. Heaven is the perfect place that God has promised to all who put their faith in his Son, Jesus.

Page 4 – John 11:35 – This verse is the shortest verse in the Bible. Jesus loves everyone and He used His time on earth to show us how much He cares. He weeps and cares for our troubles and sorrows, and He loves us so much that He even died for all our sins; He died for us! Wow! After He died, He rose again to life and conquered death so that He could give everyone the opportunity to spend eternity with Him.

Page 5 – Matthew 18:1–5 – When children believe, they have so much love and faith while adults seem to need evidence for everything. The truth is, there is plenty of evidence in history and in the Bible that proves Jesus is who He says He is. As Christians, we can be confident that God will accomplish His plan for eternity for those that put their trust in Jesus.

Page 6 – Psalm 34:15 – Our righteousness comes from our faith in what Jesus did for us, and that alone. Therefore, when we cry out to Him, He always responds to comfort us and guide us, assuring us that we are a part of the family of God.

Page 7 – Psalm 34:17–18 – God promises us that even if sickness or death should come, He will lift us up and give us eternal life.

Page 8 – Revelation 21:3–4 – In this life, there will be tears, fears, sorrow, pain, and even death. But in Heaven, all these things will be no more. Instead, there will be a new Heaven and a new earth, and eternal life with the King of Glory.

Page 9 – Isaiah 40:31 and Philippians 3:20–21 – God can give us hope in the darkest of times, and knowing His Word will comfort us.

Page 10 – Ecclesiastes 3:1–8 and II Corinthians 5:1 – There is a time for everything, but when someone you love is gone, the pain and memories will always be a part of you. The good news is God is faithful and true. A new Heaven and a new body are coming soon; we can count on it!

Page 11 – Psalm 40:1–3 – Waiting for answers to prayer is not easy. Be patient! God hears us and He knows our every need. When someone we love passes away, we can be comforted knowing that

Page 12 – John 15:7–9 – Staying close to God assures us that God hears our prayers. Ask, the Bible says, so that God can be glorified

Page 13 – Luke 6:21 – Blessings come from knowing God's Word One day, all our weeping will turn to joy when we see our Lord and Savior face to face and know that all He promised is true.

Page 14 – I John 5:13 – God's Word promises us a place where we will live for eternity. We will have a new body, a new life, and a new home prepared for us to live where we will live forever and ever

Page 15 – John 1:12 – Have you asked God to forgive your sins? We all have them. Do you believe Jesus paid the price for sin? God will forgive us because of our faith and trust in what Jesus did. Ask Him into your heart, then believe in God as your Father.

Page 16 – Philippians 4:6–7 and Revelation 7:17 – God gives us a peace that is beyond all understanding. He comforts us especially in the hardest times.

Page 17 – Psalm 103:11–14 – There is a reason the Bible uses the word 'Father' to describe God. No other religion describes God that way. God loves you so much, like a good Father, we can go to Him at any time, for any reason, without fear.

Page 18 – John 3:16 – God showed His love for humanity in the most dramatic way possible – He gave up His only Son for us!

Page 19 – Romans 10:9–11 – God longs for us to call on His name for help and salvation. Call on the blessed name of the Son of God and put all your faith in Jesus.

Page 20 – I John 3:1 – This verse speaks for itself: "See what love the Father has lavished on us, that we should be called the children

Printed in the United States
by Baker & Taylor Publisher Services